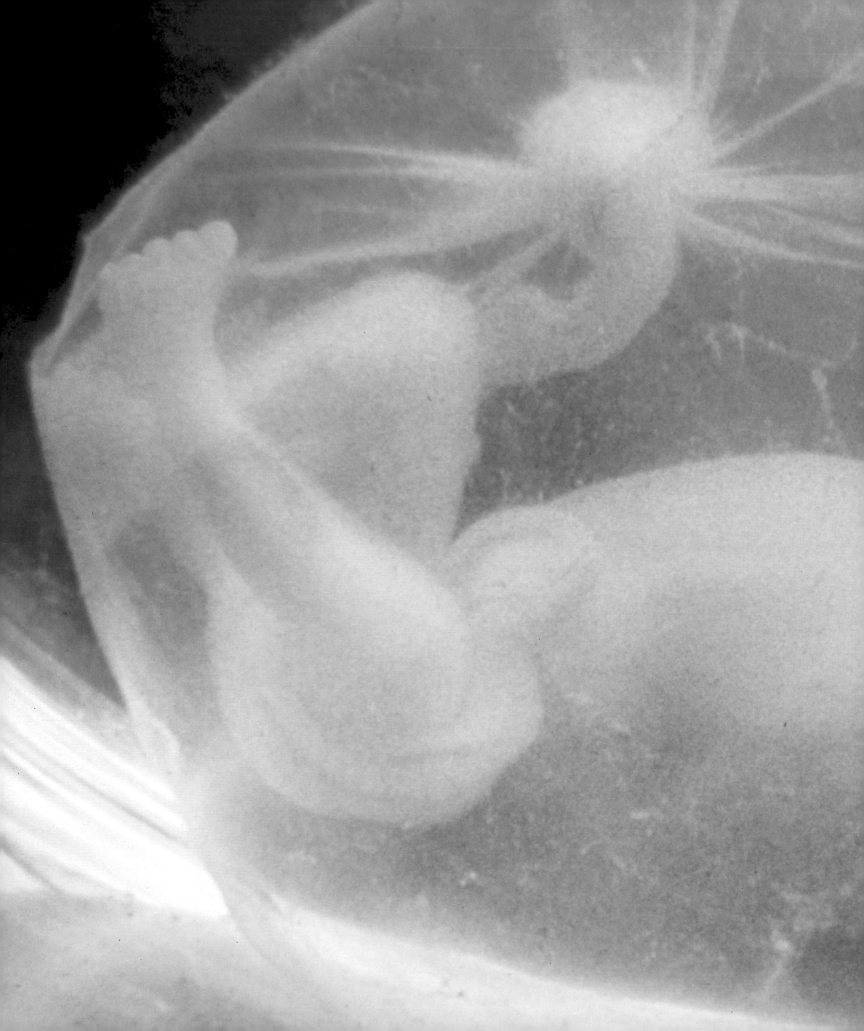

BABY

NICOLE TAYLOR

CREATIVE EDUCATION

*Designed by Rita Marshall
with the help of Thomas Lawton*

*First published in 1994 by
Creative Editions
123 South Broad Street,
Mankato, Minnesota 56001
Creative Editions is an imprint
of The Creative Company. This title
is published as a joint venture
between The Creative Company and
American Education Publishing.*

*Photography by Peter Arnold, Inc.
(Helmut Gritscher), FPG
International (Joe Baker, A.M.
Siegelman), International Stock
Photo, Lennart Nilsson (A Child is
Born, Dell Publishing Co.), Photo
Researchers (Petit Format, James
Stevenson) and Visuals Unlimited*

*Library of Congress
Cataloging-in-Publication Data*

*Taylor, Nicole.
Baby / by Nicole Taylor.
ISBN 1-56846-089-9
1. Gestation—Juvenile literature.
2. Embryology, Human—Juvenile
literature. 3. Fetus—Diseases—
Juvenile literature.
[1. Embryology, Human.
2. Fetus.] I. Title. 92-41338
RG525.5.T38 1993 CIP
612.6'3—dc20 AC*

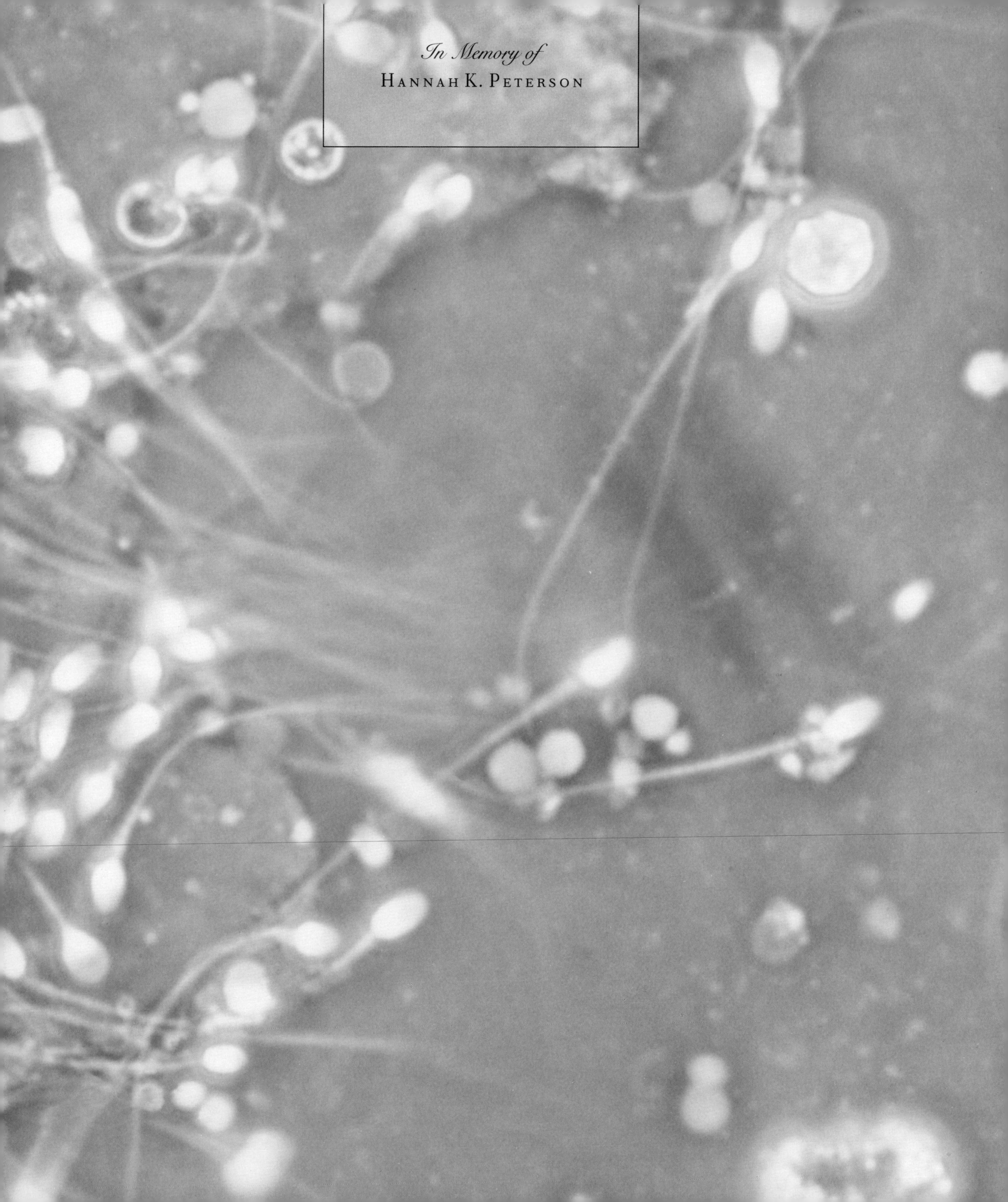

In Memory of

HANNAH K. PETERSON

Our world is inhabited by a vast number of people, all different from one another. We may be male or female, tall or short, fat or thin, blond or brunette or bald. Our skins range in color from the palest white to the deepest black. We work at different jobs, practice different customs, and speak different languages.

❧

And yet, despite our great diversity, there are countless experiences we share. Among them is the way in which our lives begin: as tiny cells uniting, dividing, growing, and changing within our mothers' bodies.

❧

Modern scientific technology now makes it possible to observe the earliest stages of life, and as a result we know more about the process of human reproduction than ever before. The more we learn, however, the more we realize that each birth is a miracle of mystery and complexity.

The hands and face of a human fetus at five months.

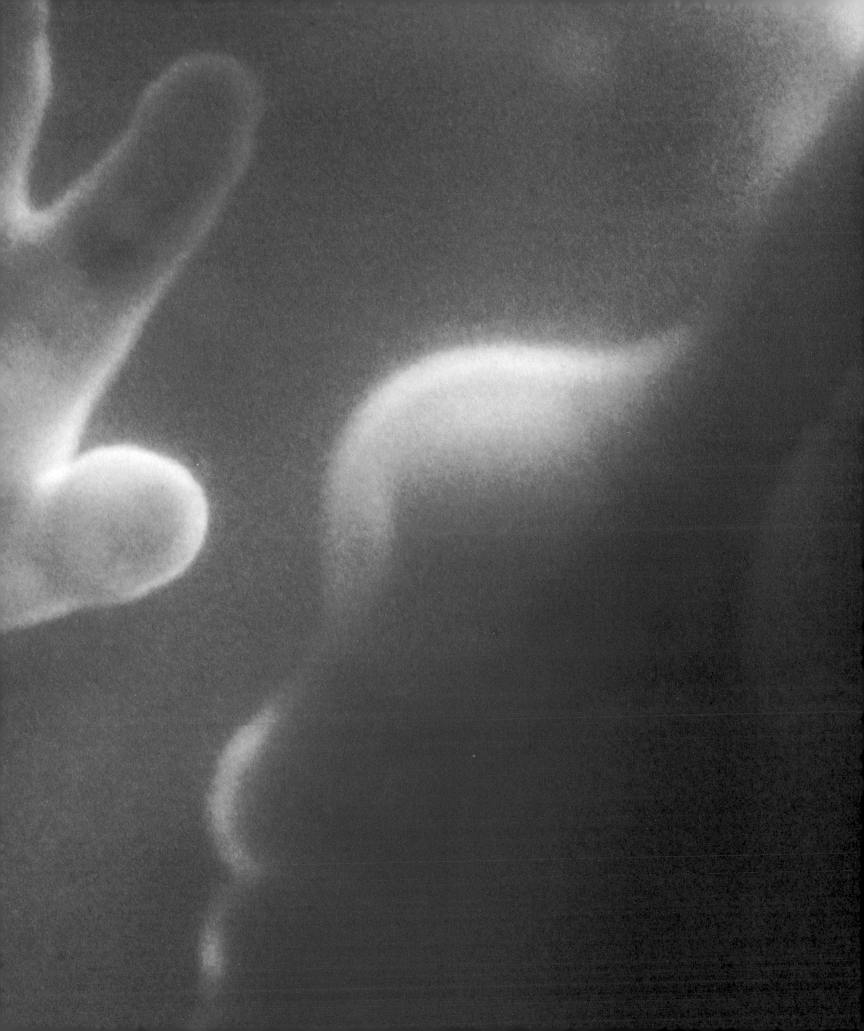

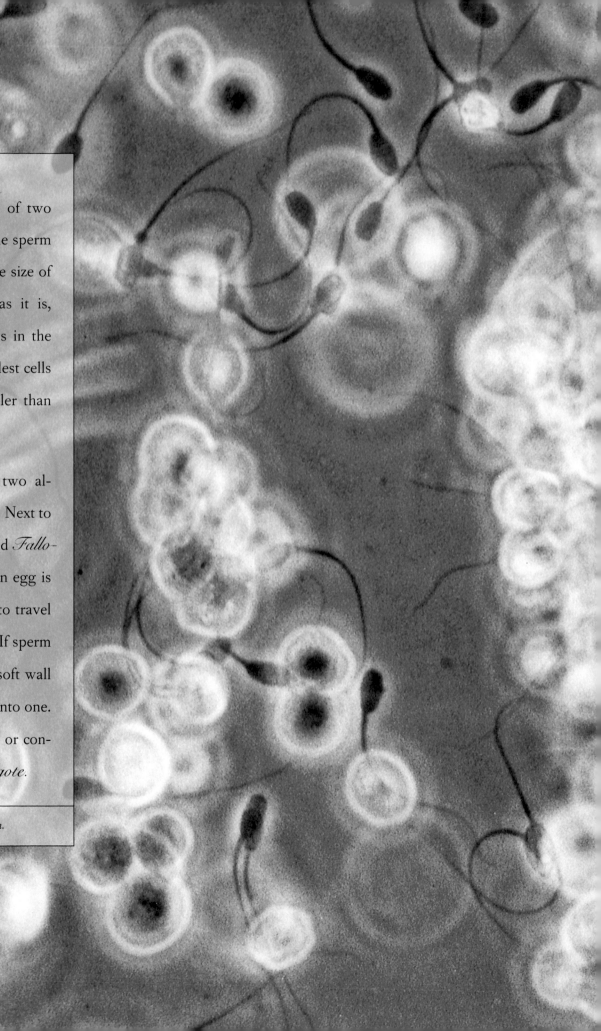

Human life begins with the fusion of two cells, the egg from the female and the sperm from the male. The *Egg* is about the size of a period on this page. As small as it is, though, it is one of the largest cells in the body. The *Sperm* is one of the smallest cells in the body. It is 2,000 times smaller than the egg.

Eggs are produced and stored in two almond-shaped glands called *Ovaries.* Next to the ovaries are tubelike organs called *Fallopian Tubes.* Once every month, an egg is released from an ovary and begins to travel through the adjacent fallopian tube. If sperm are present, one may penetrate the soft wall of the egg, and the two cells merge into one. This process is called *Fertilization,* or conception. The new cell is called a *Zygote.*

A micrograph of an egg surrounded by sperm.

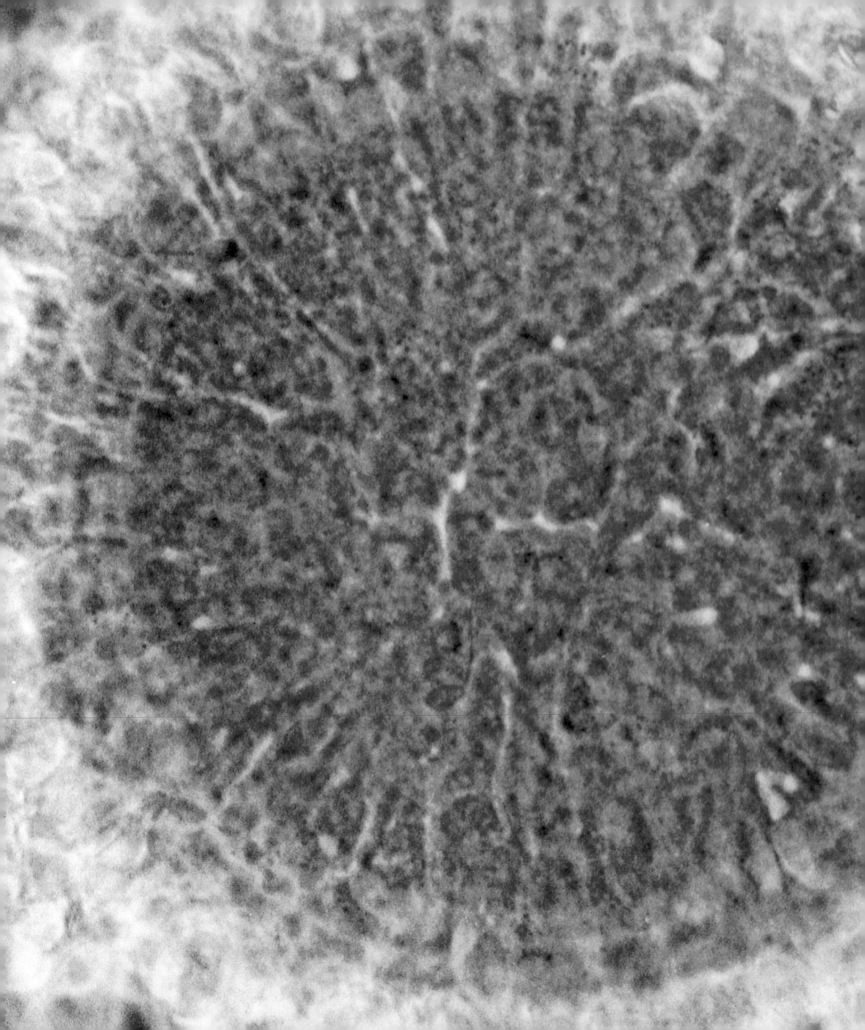

Within the next 24 hours, the zygote will divide into two cells. Further cell divisions soon follow, and when the cell mass reaches around 16 cells it is known as an *Embryo*. Each new cell contains all the genetic information present in the original fertilized egg. This information is contained in rod-shaped bodies called *Chromosomes*. The chromosomes carry all the inherited characteristics that determine physical traits such as hair and eye color and body build.

Occasionally, this cell mass splits and two or more embryos develop. If the cell mass splits in two, these embryos become identical twins, because they have the same sets of chromosomes. If two separate eggs are fertilized by different sperm, these babies will have different sets of chromosomes and are called fraternal twins.

Sperm approaching and penetrating an egg.

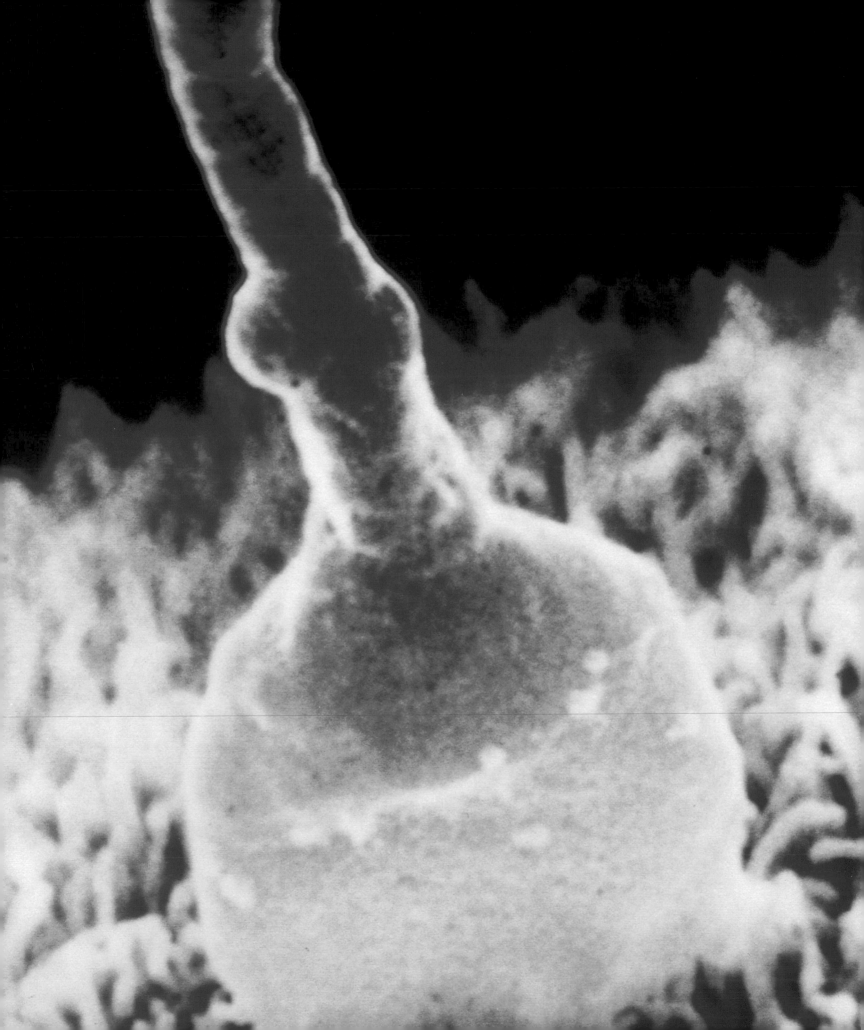

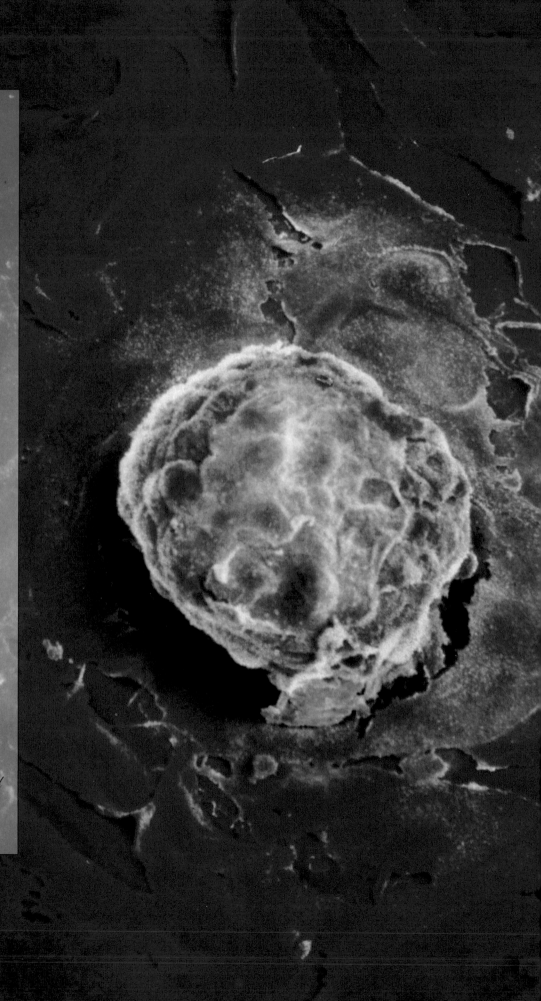

During the first week of life, the embryo slowly moves down the fallopian tube toward the *Uterus*. The uterus is a strong, hollow, pear-shaped organ that will hold the developing child until birth. In a process called *Implantation*, the embryo attaches itself to the lining of the uterine wall.

Five or six days after implantation, the uterine lining begins to erode, forming small holes like those in a sponge. The embryo's outer membrane forms rootlike extensions that attach to these holes. Together the roots and the eroded uterine lining form the *Placenta*. Its function is to exchange nutrients, oxygen, and waste between the mother and the developing child.

As the embryo grows, so does the placenta. After one month, it fills about one-fifth of the uterus; after five months it fills about half of the uterus. A tube called the *Umbilical Cord* connects the placenta to the body of

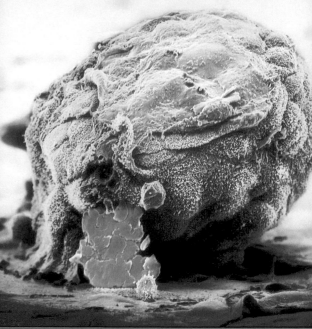

13

the child. The umbilical cord holds two fetal arteries and one fetal vein.

❧

Sometimes *Miscarriages*, or spontaneous abortions, occur. This can happen when the placenta does not function properly or when the baby's development is abnormal. About 10 to 20 percent of all pregnancies result in miscarriage, and most of these occur within the first three months of pregnancy.

Now consisting of several hundred cells, the embryo is implanted into the lining of the uterus.

Two and a half weeks after conception, the cells of the embryo form two distinct layers, the ectoderm and the endoderm. These layers will eventually give rise to different groups of tissue and organs. The *Ectoderm* will form the skin, brain, spinal cord, and nervous system. It will also form the eyes, inner ears, and teeth enamel, and the lining of the nose, mouth, and anus. The *Endoderm* will form the digestive tract,

The embryo three weeks after conception.

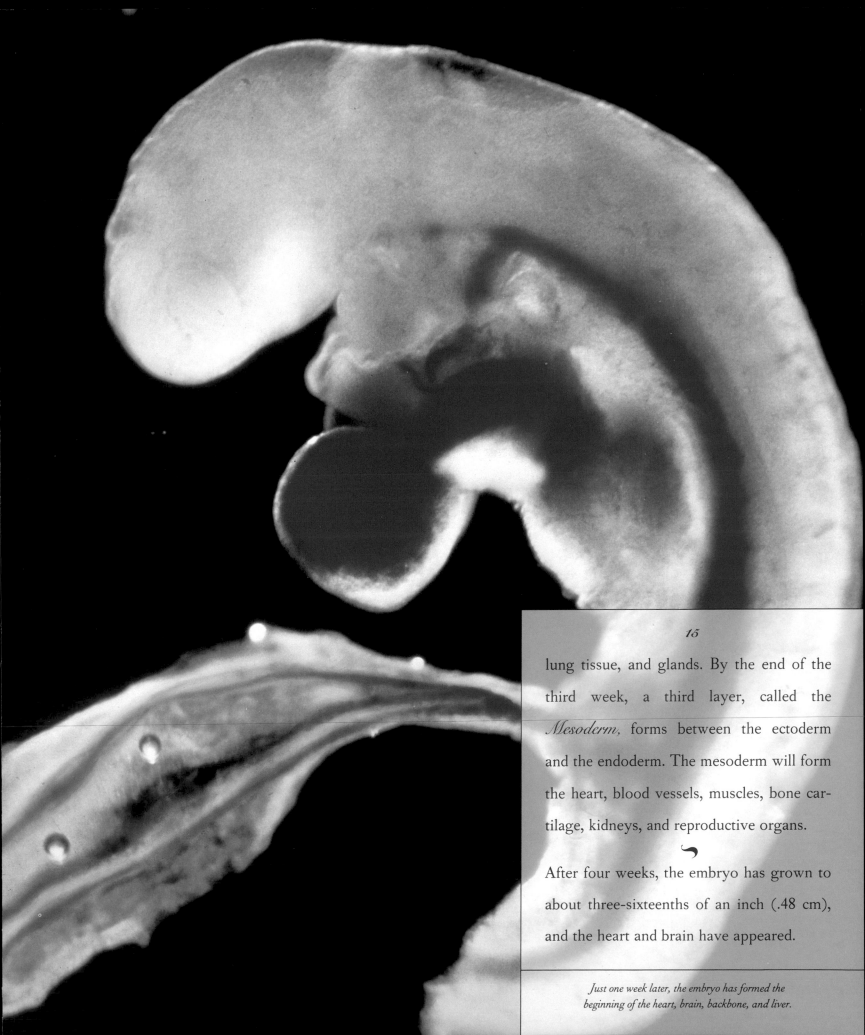

15

lung tissue, and glands. By the end of the third week, a third layer, called the *Mesoderm,* forms between the ectoderm and the endoderm. The mesoderm will form the heart, blood vessels, muscles, bone cartilage, kidneys, and reproductive organs.

↝

After four weeks, the embryo has grown to about three-sixteenths of an inch (.48 cm), and the heart and brain have appeared.

Just one week later, the embryo has formed the beginning of the heart, brain, backbone, and liver.

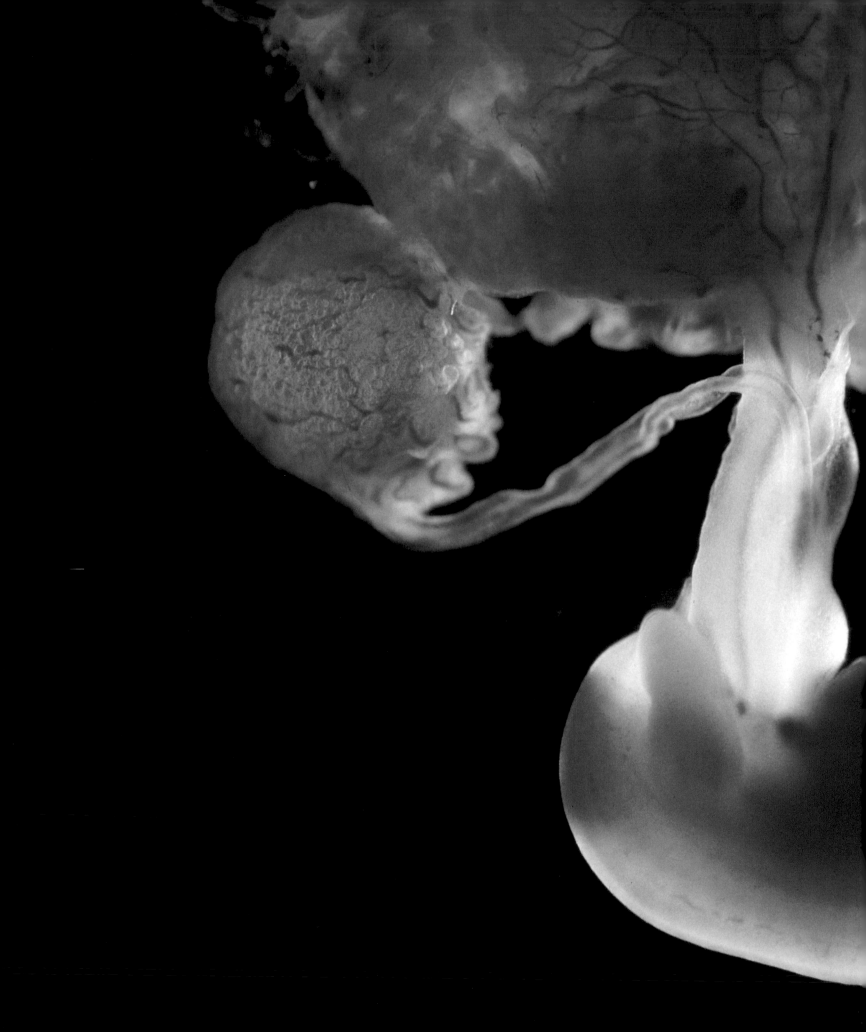

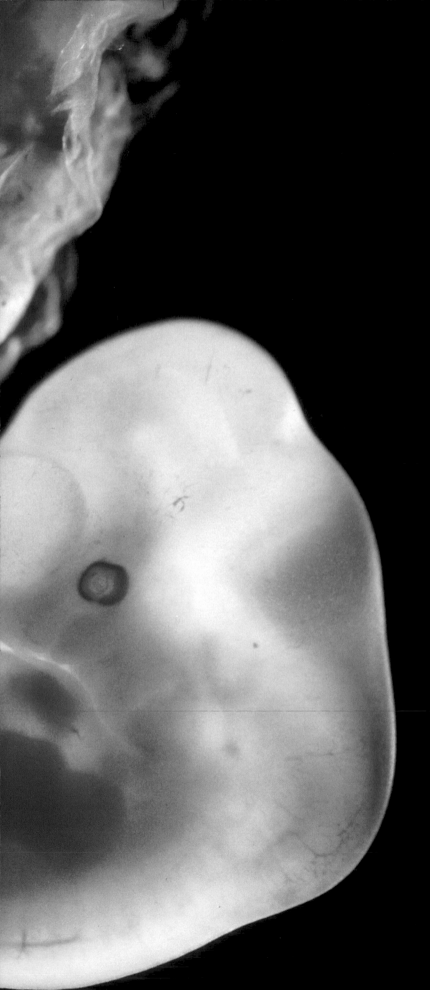

At the end of five weeks, the heart has begun pumping blood, even though the individual chambers have not yet developed. The embryo's body is curved into a C shape. About one-third of its length is the head, and it also has a tail. The arm and leg buds form, slits known as *Gill Clefts* appear where the ears will develop, and the outline of the eyes can be detected.

The embryo, placenta, and yolk sac at five weeks.

After six weeks, groups of muscles become visible. A small skeleton begins to form out of cartilage. The face and neck develop, the jaw forms, and the eyes have color. The tiny heart has divided into chambers. It beats twice as fast as the mother's heart.

During the seventh and eighth weeks, the developing child begins to resemble a human being. Ears form out of the gill clefts, and the tail becomes less obvious. Fingers and toes appear on the hands and feet, and simple reflexes begin to be evident. The embryo is still only one inch (2.54 cm) long, yet by the end of the second month, all the internal organs have formed.

Six weeks after conception, the hands and feet have begun to emerge.

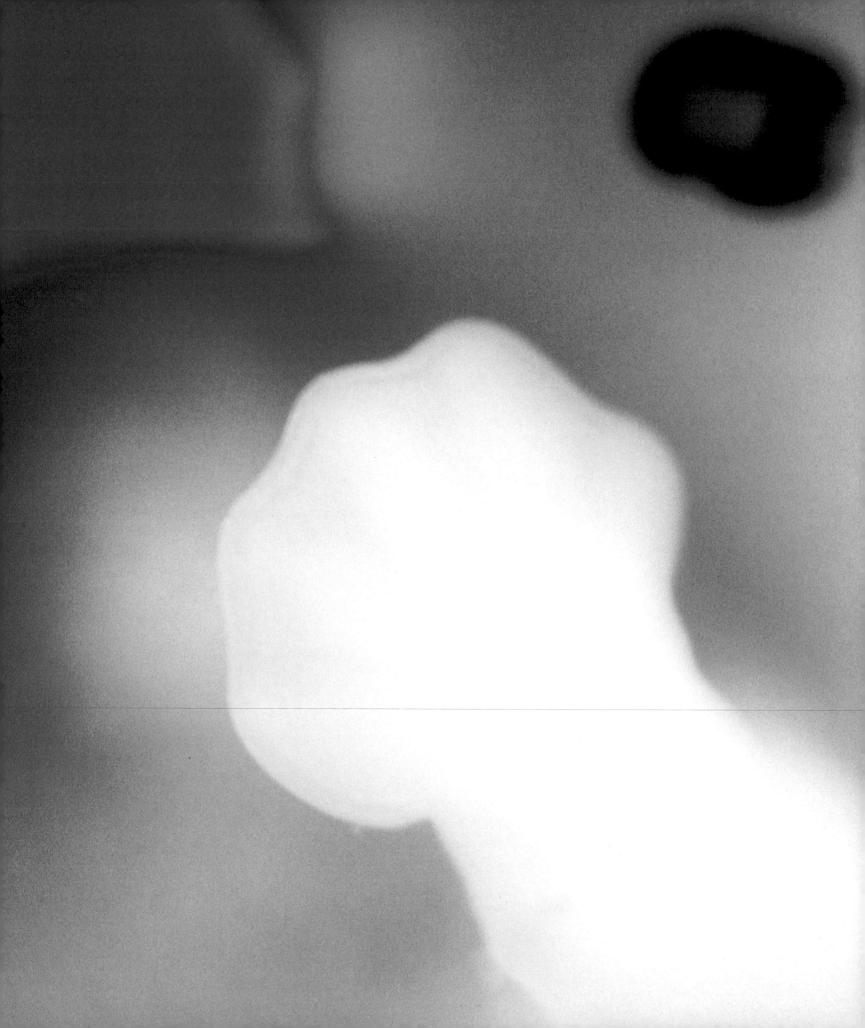

21

The child has now reached the *Fetal Stage*. The head makes up almost half the fetus. The arms, legs, fingers, and toes take on the proportions found in a baby. Bones begin to replace cartilage, and the skeleton begins to harden. External sex organs are visible.

At eleven weeks, the fetus can already open its mouth and move its arms and legs.

22

During the *Third Month,* the rate of fetal growth increases dramatically. The fetus doubles in length, and its weight more than triples. Changes within the face make it appear more human. The eyes change position from the side of the head to the front, and little earlobes become visible. Fine details such as fingernails, toenails, and hair materialize. Tooth sockets and small buds that will become teeth form in the jawbones. A fetal heartbeat is loud enough to be heard with a doctor's stethoscope. Earlier, blood had been manufactured in the liver and spleen. Now it is manufactured in the bone marrow.

By the twelfth week of development, the bones of the hands and arms have become visible.

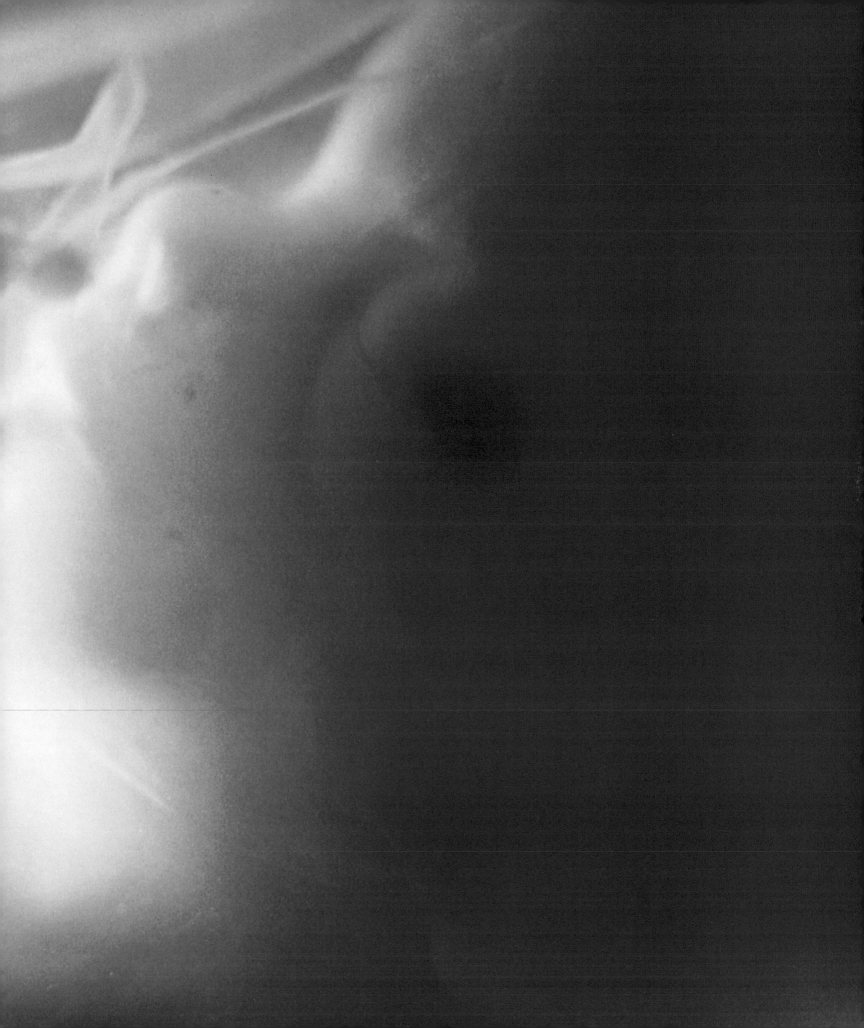

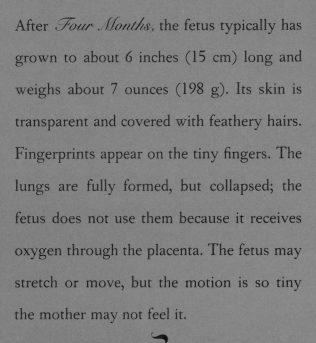

After *Four Months,* the fetus typically has grown to about 6 inches (15 cm) long and weighs about 7 ounces (198 g). Its skin is transparent and covered with feathery hairs. Fingerprints appear on the tiny fingers. The lungs are fully formed, but collapsed; the fetus does not use them because it receives oxygen through the placenta. The fetus may stretch or move, but the motion is so tiny the mother may not feel it.

After *Five Months,* the mother can easily feel the fetus move. Its heartbeat may be heard without the aid of a stethoscope. It will sleep and even hiccup. But while the fetus appears to be a complete child, the lungs, skin, and digestive tract are not normally strong enough for it to survive if born at this time.

The fetus at four months. The bubble that surrounds it is the amniotic sac, which is filled with fluid that cushions the fetus and keeps it warm.

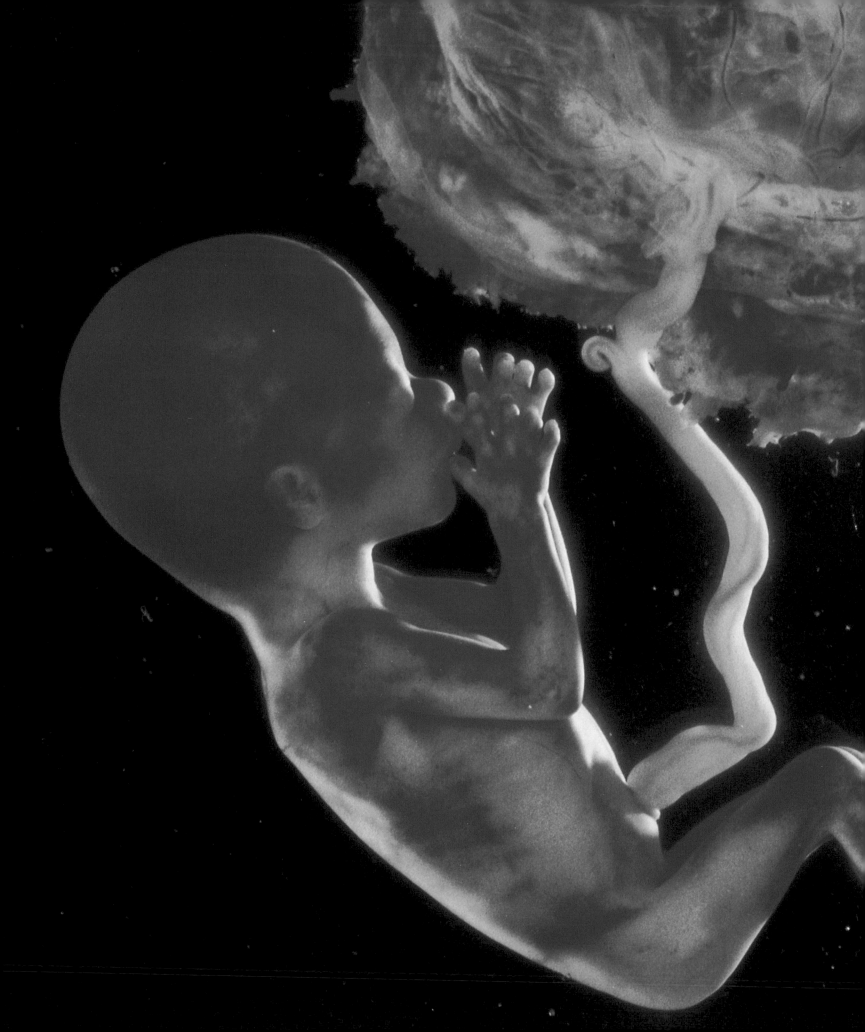

After *Six Months,* the fetus is approximately a foot (30.5 cm) long and weighs about 1½ pounds (.7 kg). All the internal organs are aligned in their correct positions. The fetus begins sucking its thumb and swallowing the amniotic fluid that surrounds it. Fine facial details, such as eyebrows and eyelashes, form. The fetal intestines fill with green pasty material composed of waste. This waste will be expelled after birth.

During the *Seventh Month,* the fetus begins storing fat. Its weight almost doubles, typically reaching 2 to 3 pounds (.9 to 1.4 kg). If born prematurely after seven months, the baby has about a 10 percent chance of survival. With the assistance of an incubator and a respirator, the baby's nervous system may be developed enough to keep its body temperature regulated and its breathing consistent.

Not alone in the womb: starting out in life as a twin.

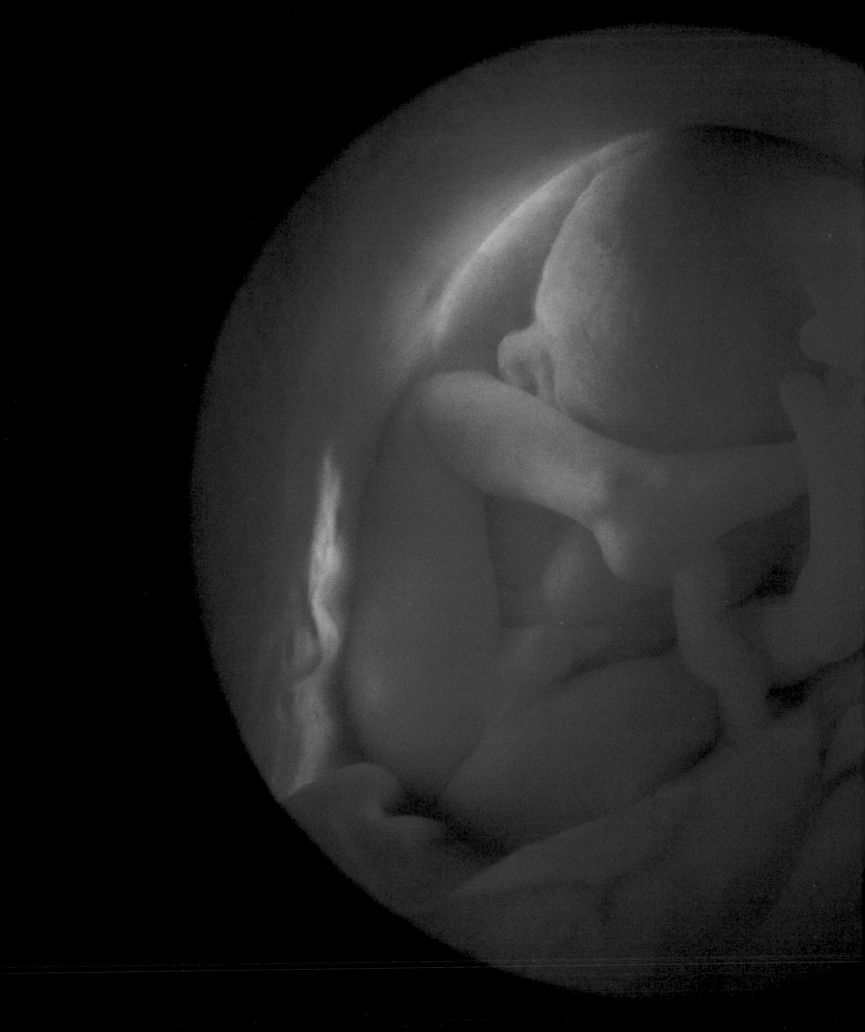

After *Eight Months,* the baby is 16 to 18 inches (41 to 46 cm) long. It has accumulated more fat and weighs 4 to 5 pounds (1.8 to 2.3 kg). The excess fat will help keep the baby warm if it is born early. The fetus can see, taste, and hear. Although the air sacs in the lungs are not fully prepared for breathing, a baby has a 70 percent chance of survival if born at this time.

During the *Ninth Month,* the fetus grows to an average of 19 to 21 inches (48 to 53 cm) and weighs between 6 and 8 pounds (2.7 to 3.6 kg). There is not much room left inside the uterus, so the fetus cannot move easily. To prepare for the impending birth, the blood in the placenta begins to clot. This blocks nutrients from passing through the umbilical cord, gradually isolating the fetus and preparing it for life outside the womb. Normally, the fetus turns so that its head faces down toward the mother's pelvis, a safe position in which to be born.

Near the end of the pregnancy, the fetus has little room to move about.

There are three stages to birth: dilation of the cervix, delivery of the fetus, and expulsion of the afterbirth. Throughout pregnancy the uterus contracts periodically. Labor doesn't actually begin, however, until the contractions occur ten minutes apart and last 40 seconds or more. During labor, the opening to the uterus, called the *Cervix*, dilates or grows wider. The uterus, the cervix, and the vagina (the tunnel leading from the cervix to outside the mother's body) join into a single tube called the *Birth Canal*. Contractions help push the baby down the birth canal.

As the second stage of birth begins, contractions occur every one or two minutes and last about one minute each. The mother has an intense need to push down. This need increases as the head of the child moves into the vagina.

The baby's head may be temporarily bent out of shape during birth. The bones are still soft and there is a gap at the top of the skull that allows the bones to overlap without injuring the infant as it pushes through the birth canal. The infant's skin is protected by a creamy coating called the *Vernix Caseosa*.

A salvelike coating called vernix caseosa shields the baby's skin during delivery.

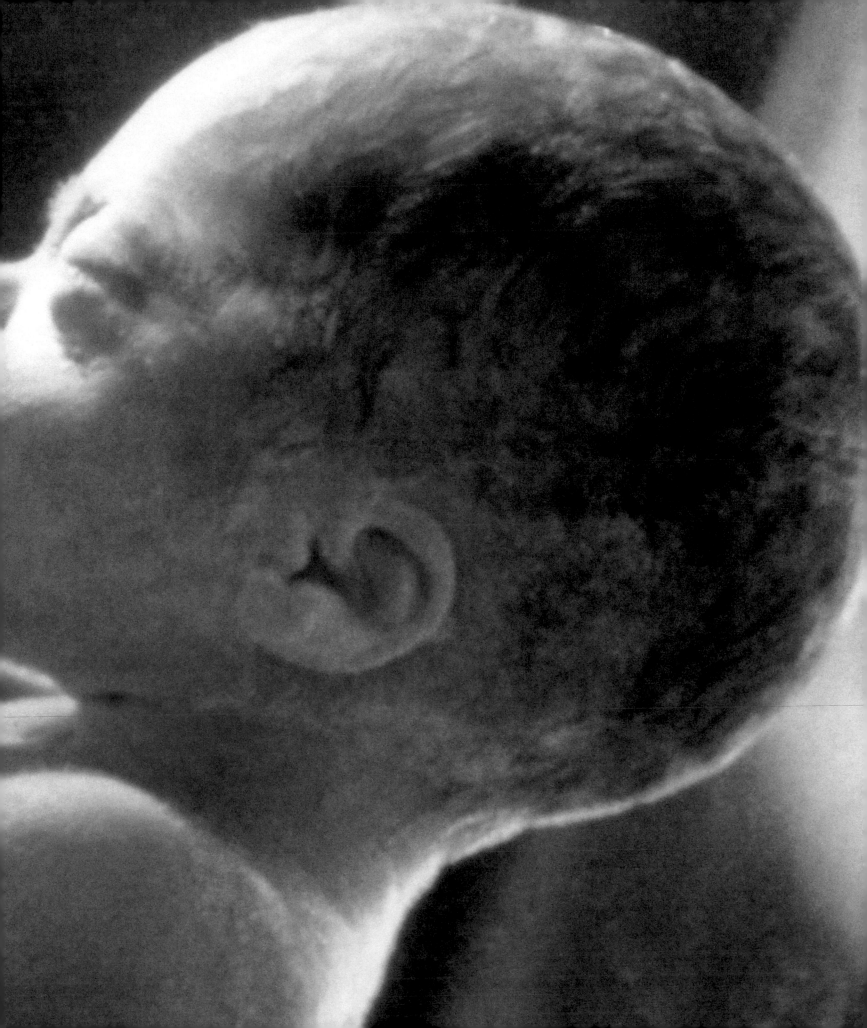

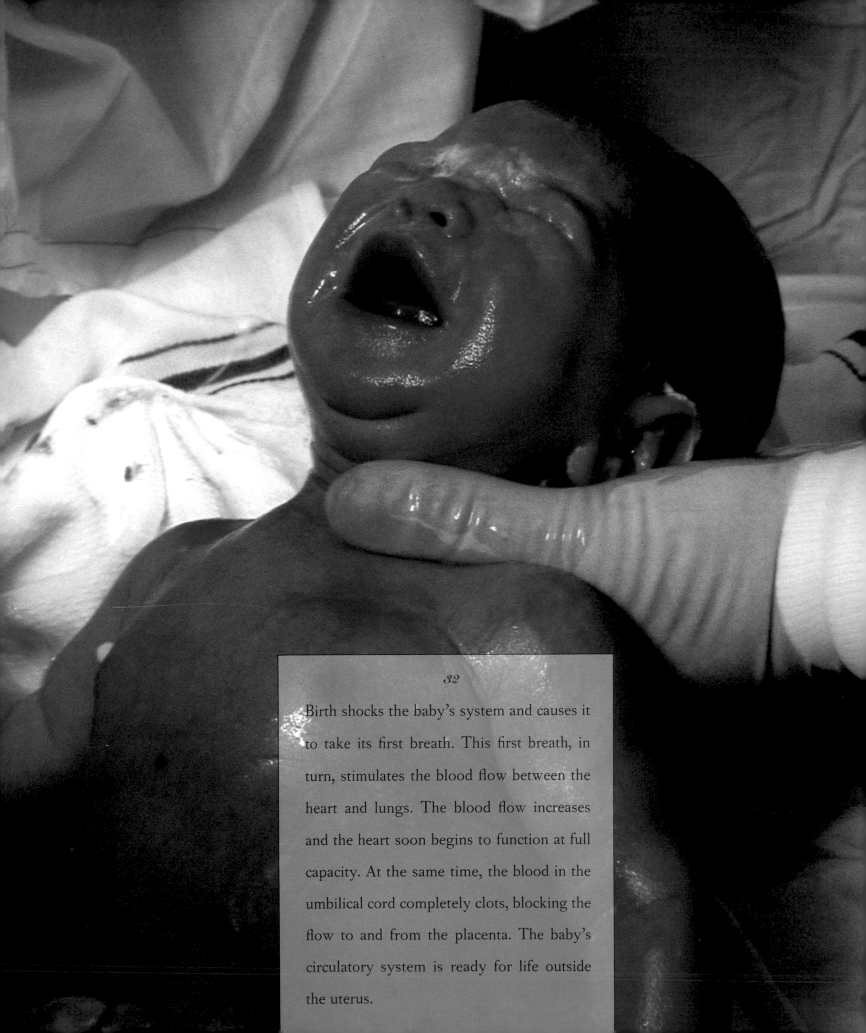

Birth shocks the baby's system and causes it to take its first breath. This first breath, in turn, stimulates the blood flow between the heart and lungs. The blood flow increases and the heart soon begins to function at full capacity. At the same time, the blood in the umbilical cord completely clots, blocking the flow to and from the placenta. The baby's circulatory system is ready for life outside the uterus.

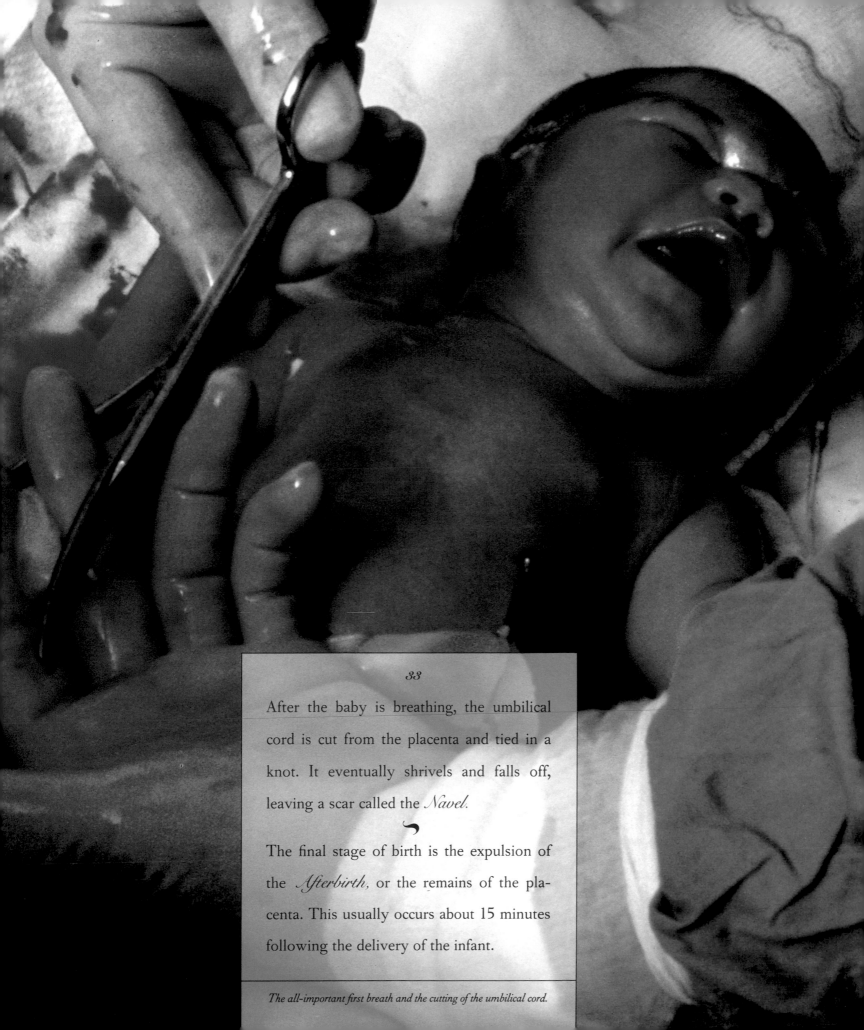

33

After the baby is breathing, the umbilical cord is cut from the placenta and tied in a knot. It eventually shrivels and falls off, leaving a scar called the *Navel*.

❧

The final stage of birth is the expulsion of the *Afterbirth*, or the remains of the placenta. This usually occurs about 15 minutes following the delivery of the infant.

The all-important first breath and the cutting of the umbilical cord.

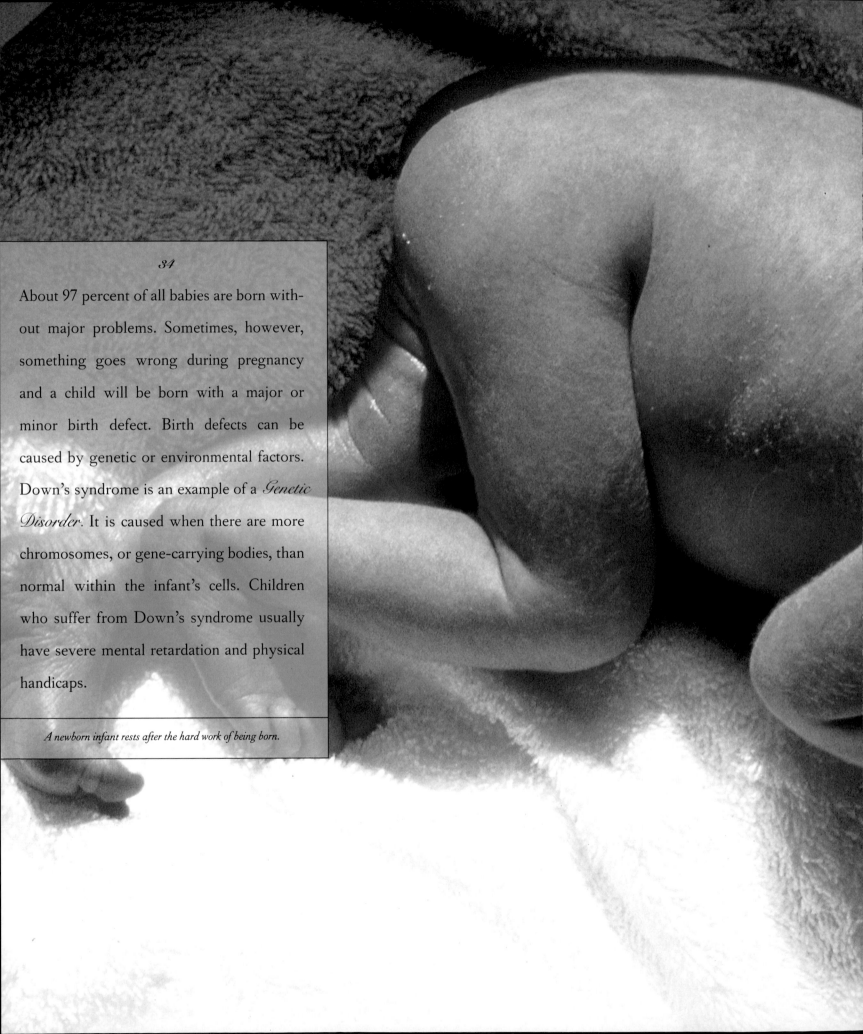

About 97 percent of all babies are born without major problems. Sometimes, however, something goes wrong during pregnancy and a child will be born with a major or minor birth defect. Birth defects can be caused by genetic or environmental factors. Down's syndrome is an example of a *Genetic Disorder*. It is caused when there are more chromosomes, or gene-carrying bodies, than normal within the infant's cells. Children who suffer from Down's syndrome usually have severe mental retardation and physical handicaps.

A newborn infant rests after the hard work of being born.

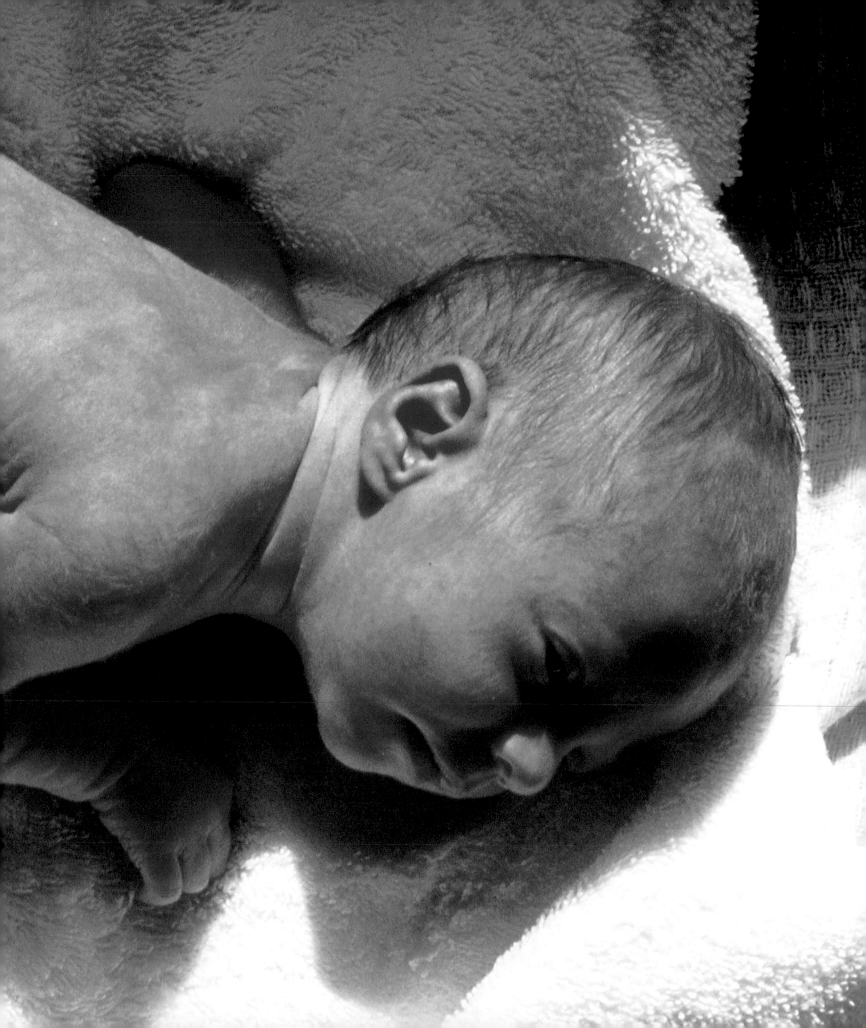

Environmental agents may also damage a developing baby. The blood of the mother and of the child never directly mix, but if a mother ingests a harmful substance, it may be passed to the child through the placenta. Damage caused in this manner is called a *Congenital Birth Defect*. One example of this occurred in the 1960s when doctors frequently prescribed a drug called thalidomide to reduce the fatigue and nausea often caused by pregnancy. The drug retarded the development of fetal limbs. Thousands of children born to mothers who took this drug during pregnancy had deformed limbs that looked like flippers.

A fetus at four months. The fine downy hair that covers it will disappear by the time of birth.

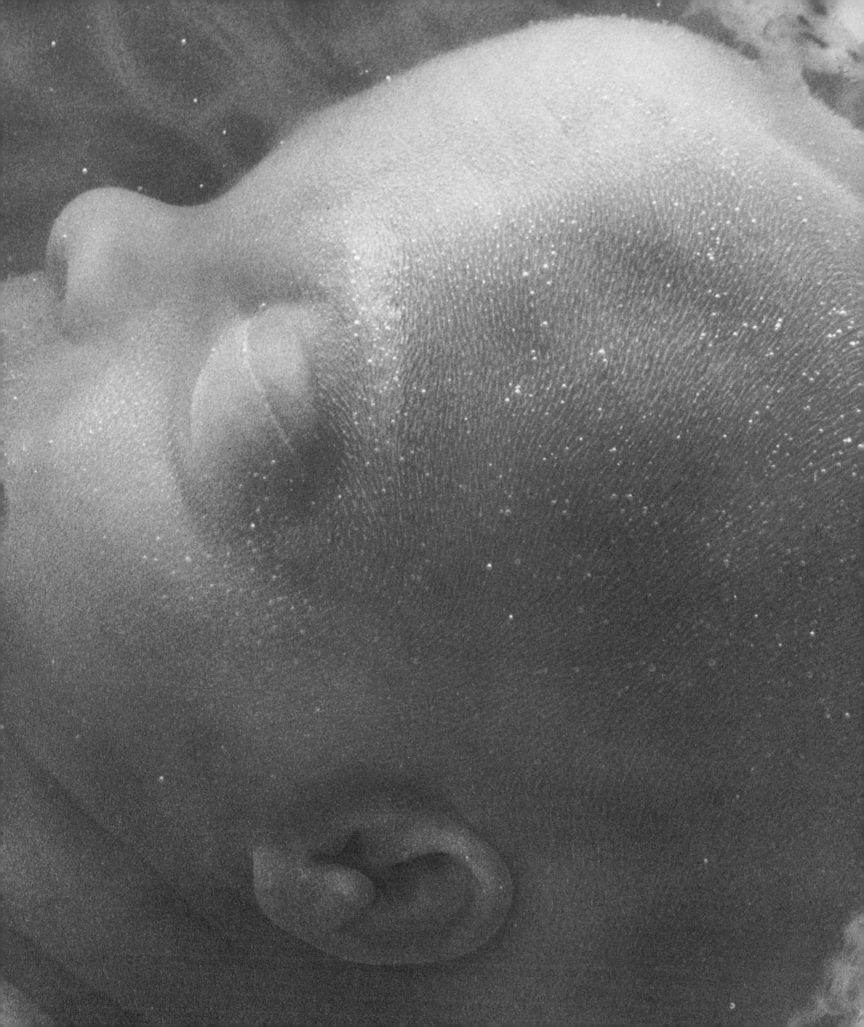

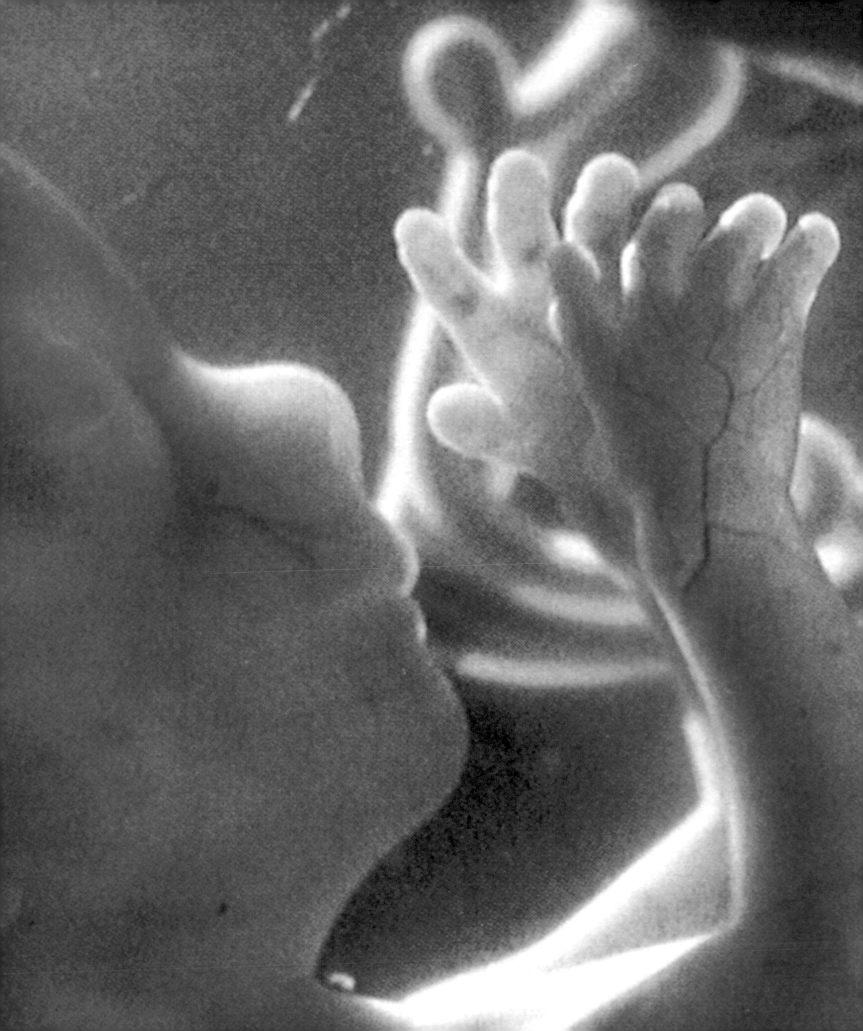

If a pregnant woman consumes alcohol, the child may be born with fetal alcohol syndrome. Children suffering from this defect have low birth weights and small heads. They may have damaged central nervous systems and be mentally retarded. Cigarette smoking during pregnancy may also affect a fetus. It frequently results in premature births and below-average IQs.

Although the mother's external environment can harm a developing fetus, with care, it can also benefit the child. For example, one study revealed that pregnant mothers who took reasonable amounts of vitamins gave birth to children with fewer birth defects. By eating a healthy diet and exercising, a pregnant woman can improve her chances of having a healthy child.

Because mother and child are linked through the placenta, a woman's lifestyle during pregnancy can have a great impact on her baby's health.

The development and birth of a *Baby* is on
of the most moving and powerful events o
our existence. Step by step, each cell fulfill
its role in shaping a new human being, com
pleting every detail as if from a blueprin
Yet an exact explanation of how life begin
is beyond current scientific understanding
Even with a population numbering in th
billions, we continue to be awed by the cre
ation of life.